AFRICAN HAIRSTYLES
BOOK II

Nonfiction

Africa Hairstyles Book II - An Historical Hair Journey

Book II First Printing June 2024
ISBN:979-8-9889305-7-0 Paperback
Published by Sula Too Publishing, Tampa, Florida
Printed in the United States.

Credits: Cover Design Background art by artist, Chris Acemandese Hall Exclusively for © Akua Adiki Anokye Publications All Rights Reserved

AFRICAN HAIRSTYLES

BOOK II

An Historical Hair Journey

By

Akua-Adiki Anokye

Sula Too Publishing, Tampa Florida

CONTENTS

INTRODUCTION

Looking back over the last 50 years of my journey, I have been compelled to try to explain "what has changed?" and "what has not?'. To be more specific this road to peace has not been a peaceful one. It has been said that we should look forward "keep our eyes on the prize", don't look back. However, how can we not look back when those constant memories keep coming to the forefront again and again and again.

17th century - slave trade

18th century - emancipation 19th century - civil rights

20th century - Black is Beautiful

21st century - hair discrimination

The struggle continues, as we are witnessing an attempt to turn back the hands of time in this country. Despite laws and attempts to not only disregard history but to rewrite history.

We must be diligent in telling OURSTORY.

Akua-Adiki Anokye   a.k.a. Shirley Singleton Mainer

MOTHER AFRICA

By Melvin I. Douglass

Oh

beautiful woman keeper of my soul

there's been so many things that have been untold

the stories of your history both young and old

> has been kept

> from my ears

> my heart my soul.

HAIRSTYLING -"AN AFRICAN ART"

"The designs of African coiffures from the simplest to the most elaborate are far too numerous to describe in general terms. Techniques include pleating, top knotting, and intricate constructions of clay, grass, string, palm and cloth. Sometimes these creations are merely held together by hair though elaborately carved combs are often used along with sticks, rods, and strips of cane to form domes and tiaras. Some tribal headdresses are so elaborate that headrests are used to keep the style intact while the weaver rests or sleeps. In some areas it is traditional to cover completed hairstyles with beautifully draped headties for travel outside the village community, to the market and for visiting friends or relatives." (1)

NIGERIA

"Women's headdressing requires a great deal of skill. Many hair arrangements are the same design in West and Central African countries, but the Yoruba women of Nigeria use the greatest variety of styles, each region having its own special way of designing and braiding. Not only do the hairstyles vary from region to region, but they also change according to the age and status of women. Special occasions call for elaborate hairdos. Priests and Priestesses and members of different religious cults often have special braided designs to set them apart from the uninitiated. These distinctions are beginning to break down however, and women are wearing whatever style they find attractive and fashionable." (2)

... "The hairstyles are innumerable each having a name and significance. They could be plaited, braided or brushed into a knot after the hair has been properly washed and dried. All weaving is done with black thread. Pomade is rubbed into the scalp before and after plaiting and braiding, which makes hair luxurious. Plaiting is done in stages. The hair is first combed finely after which it is parted into parallel lines. Few strands are worked into the braids section by section. The various braids are finally arranged and packed in various ways according to the desired style.

Styles commonly worn include "Suku", when the braids are packed and knotted at the center of the head, "Adisipako" when the hair is lumped in the back of the head, "Kolese when there are no lower braids and "Igbin Ngungi" when each braid is tied into small circles at the center of the head... Hairdressing for women has been a traditional occupation and pastime for Nigerians from time immemorable, with families, with families handing down the skill from generation to generation... (3)

SUDAN

"Nuba girls remove all hair from their body and most of it from the head. This probably for reasons of cleanliness since this area of the Nuba mountains is very dusty. Since they have well proportioned heads, the lack of hair no longer in any way disfigures their faces: on the contrary it makes them even more expressive. But they do leave a slight growth on their head and then cut decorative patterns into the short hair with great skill and imagination, making circles, geometric shapes and small ornamental tufts. The Nuba call these hairstyles MANGA. They are further evidence of the artistic sense of the Nuba." (4)

KENYA

"Although the African concept of beauty often differ from European ideas, men in Africa look for it in their women and women aim to satisfy it. Their hair seems the most difficult problem, because it is so crinkly and thick, the head is usually shaven and kept very short with the exception of the Bajun women, who often let their hair grow and braid it into thick short plaits, and the Boran whose women wear hair in hundreds of tiny thinly plaited braids which hang to the shoulders causing them to undergo a very painful process of hairbraiding by which that hair is pulled and stretched so as to straighten it, enabling it to be braided from the roots... " (5) The Masai women of Kenya have little or no hair, but adorn themselves heavily with beads. It is the young Masai warriors who go through great lengths in the styling of their hair. They oil and pad their hair with ocher, then it is made into small plaits which hang loose and are tied into knots to form different styles. It is not unusual for these young warriors to spend an entire day doing each other's hair.

SOUTHWEST AFRICA

The Bushman woman of South Africa wear their hair very short and cropped close to the head. They do decorate their head with long strands of beads which hang loose around the head, medallions and other metal ornaments are often found hanging on the loops. Some of the women choose very intricately designed bands to wear around the head.

CONGO

The Watusi women appear to have cone shaped heads. This is said to be the result of having their heads tightly bound at birth (some say to gain height, since their men grow naturally to heights of seven to eight feet). The process also trains their hair to grow straight upward. The hair is neatly trimmed, and a decorative band is worn around the forehead, giving the appearance of a crown, like that of the ancient Egyptians.

GHANA

Many of the women of Ghana are usually seen wearing headties which are part of their traditional dress. When the women take off these. headties we can find some of the most beautiful style of hairwrapping. The hair is parted into intricate shapes and patterns and then each individual section is very tightly wrapped with black thread down to the very ends. All the ends are then connected to form eloquent dimensional "works of art" in the form of crowns or what might appear to be netting from afar. Also, the ends could be knotted then shaped into a tree silhouette or a grouping of curls or waves.

HAIRBRAIDING & IT'S AFRICAN AMERICAN HISTORY

By Sandra Robinson

The origin of the cultural traditions surrounding hair braiding was explored by Hairstylist/ Carla S. Brown, at the Queens Borough Public Library in Astoria during a recent celebration of Black History Month.

Committed to having the art form of braiding recognized and preserved as a viable hairstyle for women, Brown a native of Harlem, has been braiding for 20 years and received her Cosmetology License in 1981 from Ultissima Beauty School in Flushing, N.Y.

Having taken several trips to Egypt and Senegal, Ms. Brown found herself intrigued by the many natural styles of the region. "In Africa braids were a form of communication that explained what was going on in one's life", she shared. According to Brown, certain styles signified puberty, pregnancy, a warrior or a widow. For example, long plaits wrapped in brass indicated a beautiful woman.

"When we first came to this country, we suffered great psychological damage in being told we had "bad hair". As a result, we did not have time to take care of hair as we did in Africa, so we began to use lye to straighten it." she said. Brown stressed that African Americans must get rid of thinking that our hair is "bad" and full of "naps" and "peas". The only time our hair is bad is when it is on the floor.

The African American women and children that attended this event were quite eager to get hands-on experience under Ms. Brown's direction. She demonstrated three techniques on mannequins... the goddess braid, the flat twist and fishtail.

According to Ms. Brown there are 500 braiding salons in Brooklyn and Queens alone. "Today Black hair is a million-dollar industry," said Ms. Brown. Since 1992, the N.Y. Cosmetology State Board has required that braiders be licensed to work in salons. "In the 1960's we witnessed the resurgence of Black pride with the Afro worn by entertainers such as Steve Wonder and Miriam Makeba, she continued. During the 1970's the movie "10" promoted braids being fashionable for other ethnic backgrounds. In the 1980's braiding salons opened up in Harlem and people from all over the world were flocking to New York to get their hair braided."

For a tradition that has lasted thousands of years, clients indicate that patience and proper maintenance are important factors to the beauty and longevity of a braided hairstyle. "Braids make your hair look nice, it's natural and you can avoid constant salon appointments." said

Michelle Vargas a student at I.S. 26 in Astoria. Angel Melvin, a Master Braider and Cosmetologist from Brooklyn, expressed "Braiding gives the hair a break, a chance to be chemical free and promotes growth."

Ms. Brown advocates teaching the art of braiding as part of a multicultural education in the school system, "teenagers love braiding, and they are at the age when they can learn very fast".

"KEEP BRAIDS ALIVE", she said.

*Reprinted from the "Directory of Braiding and Natural Hair Stylists/Salons" BRAIDER'S GUIDE II - 1995 AKUA-ADIKI

BRAIDING GLOSSARY - A-Z

Bantu knots - box braids are made into individual knots on the head Box braid - created by parting the hair into squares, then braiding each section.

Braids - to interweave multiple strands of hair to form a single braid.

Buffruto -strands of hair are tied in intervals then pushed up to form puffs or balls.

Cassamas - inverted braid (more hair can be added) to make it flat and stiff edges singed to keep from unraveling.

Coils - small sections of wet hair made into spirals using the end of a fine-tooth comb.

Corkscrews - patches of hair are wrapped with thread in a spiral leaving open spaces, then the thread is pulled and knotted.

Cornrows - as you are braiding additional hair is gathered so that the braid is now molded flat on the head in rows.

Dreadlocks - also known as "dreads" or "locs" are rope like strands of hair formed by natural matting (not combing) over time the hair will "lock".

Flat twist - while twisting several strands hair is gathered close to the scalp to get a kind of twisted cornrow.

Fishtail braid - four section of hair are entwined instead of the usual three.

Fulani braids - a style combining cornrows in the front half and box braids in the back half of the head.

Goddess braid - hair is added to form thick cornrows which are then shaped on the head, sometimes to form a crown.

Locks - also called "dreadlocks" which is the natural locking of uncombed hair, there are many variations of 'locs' (e.g....nu-locks, Nubian locks, African locks, Sister-locs) begin by twisting or palm rolling the hair.

Micro braids - braiding very few strands into very tiny braids. Plaiting   - what is now referred to as braiding or cornrows.

Pixie braids - short individual braids or twists to which hair is added.

Senegalese twists - African wool called "lin" is added to the hair as an extension, then twisted and knotted on ends.

Silky dread - wrapping braids or locks with different colors and types of threads.

Twists - two sections of hair are twisted together then hang freely.

Wrapping - heavy thread or hair or yarnis used to wrap section of hair very tightly from the scalp to the ends, then connected to form arches or intricate shapes.

NATURAL HAIR CARE TIPS

1. Keep hair and scalp clean, wash hair bi-weekly. Excessive washing will dry out natural oils, causing dull limp hair.

2. Keep hair and scalp oiled. Coconut oil is one of the best for proper hair care. Dry hair becomes brittle due to lack of oil and is more likely to split and break.

3. Brush hair with a natural brittle brush, do not use nylon or synthetic hairbrushes (they tear out the hair) brushes help to distribute natural oils evenly down the strands of hair.

4. Proper diet is also important to remember. hair substance is composed of iron, oxygen, hydrogen, carbon sulfur and directly affects the condition of the hair. Protein nourishes the hair.

5. Do not straighten or press your hair. Pressing with hot combs, burns out the natural oils. Chemical straightening is even more detrimental, can cause sores and permanently damage hair roots.

6. Keep hair cornrowed, braided or wrapped as often as possible. Not only is it stylish, but helps the hair grow and protected from abuse.

7. ALWAYS HAVE A POSITIVE ATTITUDE ABOUT YOUR HAIR.

HOW TO GROW LOCKS

(THE NATURAL CURL OF OUR HAIR)

1. Naturally Letting the hair go (grow) as it springs forth from your head.

2. Guiding Twisting the hair by crisscrossing it together as it were twine or rope.

3. Braiding Plaiting or braiding the hair and letting them grow into locks.

The natural curl of our hair will always grow into locks (long curls) when we stop combing or putting chemicals in it! The kinkier your hair is the quicker the natural process takes place. If your hair is straight, the locking process takes longer.

We have witnessed how beautiful hair can be when we give it the opportunity to grow and flow freely in its natural state without combs or chemicals. Allowing the hair to grow into locks causes no tension on the hair shaft or brain since there is no combing or pulling on the hair. This allows the hair to grow long, healthy and beautiful.

Twists (crisscrossed, rope style) stretch the hair and allow it to grow in a set style, pattern, thinness or thickness while growing into locks (it's natural curl).

When twists are chosen, one has many choices of style. Twists can be formed thick or thin, big or small. If you twist your hair to thin, however, it could cause breakage when the hair begins to lock and grow long.

Locks can also be formed by braiding the hair and letting it grow into locks. Braids stretch and group the hair together. This allows the hair to grow long and eventually out into locks. Braids can be big or small depending on the desired look.

Because our hair can pick up lint, it is necessary to groom it regularly. Take care to do this in the early stages of locking or lint might become deep set within your hair. If you do have lint that is lodged in your hair, don't pick it out unless it's near the surface. Nine times out of ten, picking deep set lint causes breakage of the lock and later because you upset the structure of the lock. Standing with your hair under the shower or waterfall helps bring lint from within the hair to the surface.

Your locks will tend to unify and grow together. If you want thin medium locks, then you might want to separate them as they grow together.

Washing your hair with aloe, cassi (cactus), shampoo or just getting your hair wet as often as you can (if the climate permits) is one of the keys to lock growth. The water helps keep your hair clean. The weight of the water helps your hair to drop down and brings lint to the surface.

Sister Adio Kuumba/PRAISES PRODUCTS

Reprinted from the Premier Issue/Braider's Guide/1994
Alcua-Adiki Anokye Publications/New York

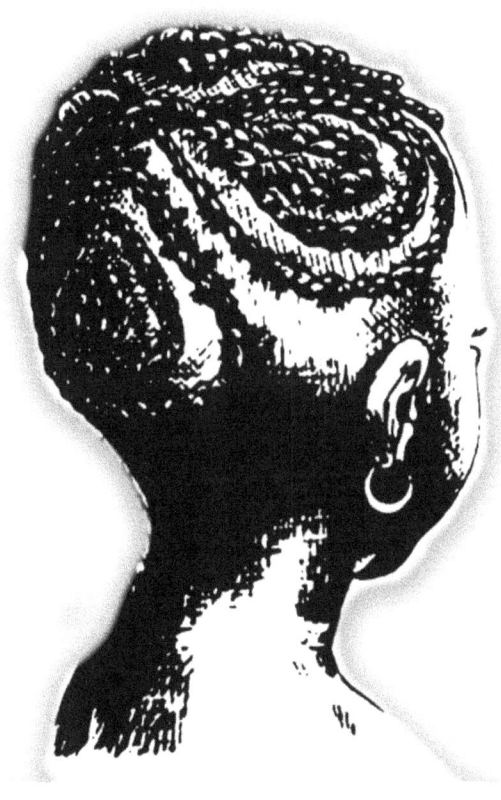

"HAIR" OURSTORY

"Our Story" - Our history

18th Century

The "Tignon Law" (also known as the chignon law) was a 1786 law enacted by the Spanish Governor of Louisiana, Don Esteban Rodriguez Miro that forced Black women to wear a tignon headscarf.

...the Spanish Governor was said to have disliked the actions some Black women who chose to show "much luxury in wearing their elaborate hairstyles, considered them a threat to the status quo, and attracted to much attention from men.

...in his decree he state that all women of color had to wear a scarf or handkerchief as a visible sign of belonging to a "slave class" whether they were slaves or not and could no longer have feathers or jewelry in their hair.

...the laws were enforced well into the 19th century, only ending after the U.S. purchased Louisiana from the French.

19th Century

Madame C.J. Walker (born Sara Breedlove) 1867-1919 was an African American entrepreneur, the first self-made female millionaire in America (according to the Guinness Book of World Records).

... she made her fortune by developing and marketing a line of cosmetics and haircare products for Black women.

...she suffered severe damage and other scalp ailments, including baldness due to skin disorders and application of harsh products to clean her hair and wash clothes (she worked as a laundress), other contributing factors included poor diet, illness, infrequent bathing and hair washing....she learned about haircare from her brothers, who were Barbers in St. Louis, MO. She later became a commissioned sales agent for Anne Turbo Malone (1869-1957) who produced the "Wonderful Hair Groomer" products and established Poro College (a cosmetology school). Malone would later become her biggest rival and accuse Sara of stealing her formula...a mixture of petroleum jelly and sulfur that had been used for hundreds of years.

...following her marriage to Charles Walker in 1906, Sara became known as Madame C.J. Walker (the "madame" was adopted from women pioneers of the French beauty industry). After moving to Pittsburg, PA. the Walkers opened a beauty parlor and established Leila College to train "hair culturists". Walkers' method of grooming was designed to promote hair growth and to condition the scalp through the use of her products. In addition to training in sales and grooming. Walker showed other Black women how to budget, build their own business and encourage them to become financially independent.

***In October of 2022 the NIH (National Institute of Health)

released a study that found that Black Women may be more affected using chemical hair straighteners.

***As of March 2024, there are 8,334 chemical hair straightening lawsuits pending.

***If you or a family member were diagnosed with uterine cancer after using chemical hair straightening products you may be eligible for compensation...

"HAIR" OUR STRUGGLES

(Hair Discrimination)

1970 - Beverly Jenkins was denied a promotion by her supervisor due to her afro hairstyle.

1978 - Pam Ferrell was fired from her job due to her braided hairstyle which led to her becoming one of the first activist in the natural hair movement.

1980 - Shirley Mainer was called in to H.R. and told that her braided hairstyle was nonprofessional and violation of company policy.

1981 - Renee Rogers brought charges against her employer after she was dissuaded from wearing her hair in cornrows.

1987 - Cheryl Tatum was told by her employer that her braided style was in violation of the companies dress code".

2010 - Chastity Jones went in for an interview, was hired and minutes later the job was rescinded due to her II dreadlocks".

2013 - Tiana Parker, a 7-year-old straight A student sent home from school in tears after being told her dreadlocks hairstyle was not presentable".

2013 - Dymon Davis arrived to work wearing her natural hair style, was pulled aside by her supervisor and told that her hair was II wild and unkept".

2017 - Deanna & Mya Cook barred from attending school activities because of their hair extensions... told that their style was distracting and therefore violated school policy.

2017 - Destiny Tompkins told by her employer that her box braid hairstyle was "too urban" for the company culture.

2018 - Faith Fennidy a sixth grader sent from school after being told that her hair extensions violated school policy.

2018 - Andrew Johnson forced to have his locs cut out during a high school wrestling match.

2018 - 6-year-old Clinton Stanley, Jr. stopped from entering school on his first day and told to cut his dreadlocks.

2019 - Brooke & April Skinner expelled from dance school for not taking out their box braids.

2019 - Kerion Washington denied employment because of his hairstyle.

2020 - Asio Simo a 17-year-old high school senior was

kicked off of the cheerleading team because of her hairstyle.

2020 - DeAndre Arnold a high school senior was told that he could not walk at graduation unless he cut his locks.

.2021 - 4-year-old Gus "Jeff Hawkins was told that his braids violated the dress code at his school.

Hair discrimination: the U.S. military

1975 - Army Specialist Babette Peyton was court marshaled for wearing "cornrows" which violated U.S. Army policy against so called "outlandish hairstyles" while serving in Germany.

In March of 2014 - the U.S. Dept. of Defense issued a set of guidelines that banned all afro's, dreadlocks, braids and twists that were greater than ¼ inch in diameter.

Changes in military policy:

2014 - U.S. Navy changed the military grooming standards to support women with braided and natural styles.

2015 - the U.S. Marine Corp. approved locks and twisted hairstyles for women marines.

2017 - U.S. Army also authorized female soldiers to wear dreadlocks.

2018 - U.S. Airforce authorized female service members to wear dreadlocks.

Hair discrimination: Canada

Viola Desmond/Canadian Civil Rights Activist (is featured on $10. bill) launched the first "hairdressing school" of its kind in Nova Scotia after being rejected by all beauty schools for being black.

2010 - Armstrong vs. Anna's Hair Spa /Ontario...she was refused service and told that they don't do black hair (she had dreadlocks).

2014 - Letitia McNickle hostess at Madison Bar & Grill was asked to leave because of her braids

2016 - Akua Agyemfre server at Astor's Bar & Grill sent home because her hair was in a bun.

2016 - Cree Ballah who worked at Zara was told that her hair did not fit the brands "clean and professional look".

2019 - Natasha Doyle-Merrick worked at an Edmonton AGO bistro and was told that her hair could "scare customers".

*McGill Journal of Law & Health-9/8/2022 blog/ Annaelle Barreau

" ... In Canada, there is a stigma and misconceptions surrounding Afro-texture hair. Beauty Schools do not include afro-texture hair in their curriculum, and there is a lack of positive representation in the main-stream media... a petition gathering 30,000 signatures to give afro-hair a place in beauty school programs... No official change has taken place... "

Hair Discrimination: in the U.K.

2014 - Simone Pouderly was asked to remove her braids by a modeling agency or risk losing a job opportunity.

2015 - Lara Odoffin a university graduate had a job offer withdrawn because she wore a braided hairstyle.

2017 - A Harrods applicant was told to straighten her natural hair or forfeit a job offer.

2017 - Chikayea Flanders a 12-year-old had to cut off his dreadlocks or face school suspension.

2019 - Josiah Sharpe a 5-year-old was banned from the playground during breaktime and sent home from school for "an extreme fade haircut".

Ruby Williams a 14-year-old was sent home from a London school for having an afro, in breach of school policy.

In 2020: *The "HALO COLLECTIVE" was founded by Edwina Omokaro, it established the "Halo Code" a pledge to be signed by schools and organizations. This was the first attempt to protect employees in the U.K. who came to work with natural and protective hairstyles.

"HAIR" OUR LAWS

THE CROWN ACT

(Creating a Respectful Open Workplace for Natural Hair)

The bill was sponsored by the "Crown Coalition", created by DOVE in sponsorship with the National Urban League, Color of Change and the Western Center on Law & Poverty. first introduced by Senator Holly J. Mitchell(D) of California and signed into law by Governor Gavin Newsome on July 3, 2019.

State Senate Bill No. 188 (see entire bill on following pages)

Other states followed: to date 23 states now have laws prohibiting "natural hair discrimination".

Alaska, Arizona, Arkansas, Colorado, Connecticut, Delaware, Illinois, Louisiana, Maine, Maryland, Massachusetts, Michigan, Minnesota, Nebraska, Nevada, New Jersey, New Mexico, New York, Oregon, Tennessee, Texas, Virginia, Washington

In March of 2021, Representative Bonnie Watson-Coleman (D-N.J.) introduced the CROWN Act, it passed in the House of Representatives 235-189, was then sent on to the Senate and

H.R.2116 is still yet to be passed in the SENATE. (see Appendix - Laws Full Text):

HAIR SHEROES (PIONEERS)

Although there are many women who have been in the forefront of the HAIR movement, I choose to highlight these two.

PAM FERRELL - after being fired from her job due to her braided hairstyle, this led her to becoming one of the first activist in the "Natural Hair Movement". In the 1980's when her Wash. D.C. base salon was being fined for opening without a Cosmetology License, she and her husband sued the D.C. gov't and as a result hairbraiding salons become exempt from Cosmetology regulations, and a separate license was created for braiders. She was appointed to the Wash., D.C. Barbers and Cosmetology Board and was pivots! in assisting the U.S. military with their review of hairstyle policies and regulations. She was instrumental in helping others with legal fees and fighting for legislative changes in other states.

DIANE BAILEY - founded with six other women the "IBN International Braiders Network". which held the first Natural Hair Care Conference in New York. She wrote the first textbook on Natural Hair & Braiding by MILADY. The IBN lobbied for the "Natural Hair Care" license in New York State. Diane designed a course to teach the art & science of natural hair and taught a "Hair Braiding Certification" course at Medgar Evers College in Brooklyn, N.Y,

Some other "Keepers of the Culture" just to name a few...

Queen Mother Moore, Black Rose, Carla Brown, Tulani Kennard, Nekhena Evans, Marion Council, Mishon Mishon, Ona Osirio Maat, Germaine Jean-Marie, Charmaine Jean-Marie, Camille Yarborough, Esi Sagay, Amazon Smiley, Ngone Sow, Taliah Waajid, Adio Kuumba, Sister Tabeel, Deborah Hare-Bey, Crystal Bailes, Cathy Jones, Sonia Bullock, Alice Henderson, June Terry, Araina Griffith Knight, Vivian Aning, Jade, Raynetta Mosley, Blessing Wilkerson, Anu Prestonia. Alicia Wilson...'

NOTES

-Poem "Mother Africa" by Melvin I. Douglass, reprinted by permission of Melvin Douglass from the book "A New Consciousness" 1977

-Jefferson, Louise F. The Decorative Arts of Africa" p. 106 reprinted by permission of Viking Press, N.Y.

-Oyawele, Femi, The Head-"Africa's Crowning Glory" p. 59 Africa Women Magazine. No. 14 Mar/ Apr 1978 reprinted by permission Harper & Row Publishers, N.Y.

Riefenstahl, Leni "The Last of the Nuba", page 18 reprinted by permission of Harper & Row Publishers, N.Y.

Ricardi, Mirella, '·shing Africa" pg. 80 reprinted by permission of William Morr &C .,N.Y.

Tignon Law: excerpt Dillman, Caroline M. (2013) Southern Woman

Madame C.J. Walker "A Brief Biographical Essay" (2020) Bundles, A'Lelia.

African Hairstyles Book I - Akua-Adiki Anokye - 1980 Braiders Guide I-A. Anokye Publications -1994 Braiders Guide - II - A. Anokye Publications - 1995

APPENDIX

Laws - Full Text

117TH CONGRESS H R2116

2D SESSION

IN THE SENATE OF THE UNITED STATES

MARCH 21, 2022

Received; read twice and refen·ed to the Committee on the Judiciary

AN ACT

To prohibit discrimination based on an individual's texture or style of hair.

1   Be it enacted by the Senate and Hoitse of Representatives of the United
    States of A1nerica in Cong1·ess assembled,

SECTION 1. SHORT TITLE.

1.   This Act may be cited as the "Creating a Respectful and Open "\\7orld for
     Natural Hair Act of 2022" or the

2.   "CRO"\\TN Act of 2022".

3.   SEC. 2. FINDINGS; SENSE OF CONGRESS; PURPOSE.

4.   (a) FINDINGS.-Congress finds the following:

5. (1) Throughout United States history, society has used (in conjunction with skin color) hair texture and hairstyle to classify individuals on the basis of race.

6. (2) Like one's skin color, one's hair has served as a basis of race and national origin discrimination.

7. (3) Racial and national origin discrimination can and do occur because of longstanding racial and national origin biases and stereotypes associated with hair texture and style.

8. (4) For example, routinely, people of African descent are deprived of educational and employment opportunities because they are adorned with natural or protective hairstyles in which hair is tightly coiled or tightly curled, or worn in locs, cornrows, twists, braids, Bantu knots, or Afros.

9. (5) Racial and national origin discrimination is reflected in school and workplace policies and practices that bar natural or protective hairstyles commonly worn by people of African descent.

HR 2118 RFS

1. (6) For example, as recently as 2018, the U.S. Armed Forces had gTooming policies that barred natural or protective hairstyles that servicemembers of African descent commonly wear and that described these hairstyles as "unkempt".

2. (7) The U.S. .Army also recognized that prohibitions ag·ainst natural or protective hairstyles that African-American soldiers are commonly adorned with are racially discriminatory, harmful, and hear no relationship to African-American servicewomen's occupational qualifications and their ability to serve and protect the Nation. .As of February 2021, the U.S. .Army removed minimum hair length requirements and lifted restrictions on any soldier wearing braids, twists, locs, and cornrows in

order to promote inclusivity and accommodate the hair needs of soldiers.

3. (8) .As a type of racial or national origin discrimination, discrimination on the basis of natural or protective hairstyles that people of .African descent are commonly adorned with violates existing Federal law, including provisions of the Civil Rights .Act of 1964 (42 U.S.C. 2000e et seq.), section 1977 of the Revised Statutes (42 U.S.C. 1981), and the Fair Housing .Act (42 U.S.C. 3601 et seq.). However, some Federal courts have misinterpreted Federal civil rights law by narrowly interpreting the meaning of race or national origin, and thereby permitting, for example, employers to discriminate against people of .African descent who wear natural or protective hairstyles even though the employment policies involved are not related to workers' ability to perform their johs.

4. (9) Applying this narrow interpretation of race or national origin has resulted in a lack of Federal civil rights protection for individuals who are criminated against on the basis of characteristics that are commonly associated with race and national origin.

5. (10) In 2019 and 2020, State legislatures and municipal bodies throughout the U.S. have introduced and passed legislation that rejects certain Federal courts' restrictive interpretation of race and national origin, and expressly classifies race and national origin discrimination as inclusive of discrimination on the basis of natural or protective hair-styles commonly associated with race and national or1gm.

6. (b) SENSE OF CONGRESS.-lt is the sense of Congress that tied into knots to form different styles. It is not unusual for these young warriors to spend an entire day doing each others hair.

1. the Federal Govermnent should acknowledge that individuals who have hair texture or wear a hairstyle that is historically and contemporarily as 4 sociated with .African .Americans or persons of African descent systematically suffer harmful discrimination in schools, workplaces, and other contexts based upon longstanding race and national origin stereotypes and biases;

2. a clear and comprehensive law should address the systematic deprivation of educational, employment, and other opportunities on the basis of2 hair texture and hairstyle that are commonly associated rith race or national origin;

3. (3) clear, consistent, and enforceable legal standards must be provided to redress the widespread incidences of race and national origin discrimination based upon hair texture and hairstyle in s c h o o l s , workplaces, housing, federally funded institutions, and other contents;

4. it is necessary to prevent educational, employment, and other decisions, practices, and policies generated by or reflecting negative biases and stereotypes related to race or national origin;

5. the Federal Government must play a key role in enforcing· Federal civil rig·hts laws in a way that secures equal educational, employment, and other opportunities for all individuals regardless of their race or national origin;

6. the Federal Government must play a central role in enforcing the standards established under this Act on behalf of individuals who suffer race or national origin discrimination based upon hair tex- ture and hairstyle;

7. it is necessary to prohibit and provide remedies for the harms suffered as a result of race or national origin discrimination on the basis of hair texture and hairstyle; and

8. it is necessary to mandate that school, workplace, and other applicable standards he applied in a ondiscriminatory manner and to explicitly prohibit the adoption or implementation of grooming requirements that disproportionately impact people of African descent.

(c) PURPOSE .-The pm1)ose of this Act is to institute   definitions   of race and national origin for Federal civilrights laws that effectuate the comprehensive scope of protection Congress intended to be afforded by such laws and Congress' objective to eliminate race and national origin discrimination in the United States.

SEC. 3. FEDERALLY ASSISTED PROGRAMS.

1. IN GENERAL.-No individual111 the United

2. States shall be excluded from participation in, be denied the benefits of, or be suQjected to discrimination under, any program or activity receiving Federal financial assistance, based on the individual's hair texture or hairstyle, if that hair texture or that hairstyle is commonly associated with a particular race or national origin (including hairstyle in which hair is tightly coiled or tightly curled, locs, cornrows, twists, braids, Bantu knots, and Afros).

3. (b) ENFORCEMENT.-Subsection (a) shall be enforced in the same manner and by the same means, including with the same jurisdiction, as if such subsection was incorporated in title VI of the Civil Rights Act of 1964 (42 U.S.C. 2000d et seq.), and as if a violation of sub-section (a) was treated as if it was a violation of section of such Act (42 U.S.C. 2000d).

4. (c) DEFINITIONS.-In this section-the term ''progTam or activity'' has the meaning given the term in section 606 of the Chil Rights Act of 1964 (42 U.S.C. 2000<l-4a); and (2) the terms "race" and "national origin" mean, respectively, ''race'' within the meaning of the term in section 601 of that Act (42 U.S.C. 2000d) and "national origin" within the meaning of the term in that section 601.

SEC. 4. HOUSING PROGRAMS.

1. IN GENERAL.-No person in the United States shall be subjected to a discriminatory housing practice   based on the person's hair teA'ture or hairstyle, if that hair texture or that hairstyle is commonly associated with a particular race or national origin (including a hairstyle in which hair is tightly coiled or tightly curled, locs, corn-rows, twists, braids, Bantu knots, and Afros).

2. ENTFORCEMENT.-Subsection (a) shall   be enforced in the same manner and by the same means, including with the same jurisdiction, as if such subsection was incorporated in the Fair Housing Act (42 U.S.C. 360113   et seq.), and as if a violation of subsection (a) was treated as if it was a discriminatory housing practice.

3. 15 DEFINITION.-In this section the terms "discriminatory housing practice"and "person" have the meanings given the terms in section 802 of the Fair Housing Act (42 U.S.C.   3602); and the terms "race" and "national origin" mean, respectiYely, "race" within the meaning· of the term in section 804 of that Act (42 U.S.C. 3604) and "national origin" within the meaning of thetcrm in that section 804.

SEC. 5. PUBLIC ACCOMMODATIONS.

1. IN GENERAL.-No person in the United States shall be subjected to a practice prohibited under section 201, 202, or 203 of the Civil Rights Act of 1964 (42 U.S.C. 2000a et seq.), based on the person's hair texture or hairstyle, if that hair textm·e or that hairstyle is commonly associated with a particular race or national origin (including a hairstyle in which hair is tightly coiled or   tightly curled, locs, cornrows, twists, braids, Bantu knots, and Afros).

2. ENFORCEMENT.-Subsection (a) shall be enforced in the same manner and by the same means, including with the same jurisdiction, as if such subsection was incorporated in title II of the Civil Rights Act of 1964, and as if a violation of subsection (a) was treated as if it was a violation of section 201, 202, or 203, as appropriate, of such Act.

3. DEFINITION.-ln this section, the terms "race" and "national origin" mean, respectively, "race" within   the meaning of the term in section 201 of that Act (42 U.S.C. 2000e) and "national origin" within the meaning of the term in that section 201.

SEC. 6. EMPLOYMENT.

1. PROHIBITION.-It shall be an unlawful employment practice for an employer, employment agency, labor   organization, or joint labor-management committee controlling apprenticeship or other training or retraining· (including on-the-job training programs) to fail or refuse to hire or to discharge any individual, or otherwise to discriminate against an individual, based on the individual's hair texture or hairstyle, if that hair texture or that hair-style is commonly associated with a particular race or national origin (including a hairstyle in which hair is tightly coiled or tightly curled, locs, cornrows, twists, braids, Bantu knots, and A.fros).

2. ENFORCEMENT.-Subsection (a) shall be enforced in the same manner and by the same means, including with the same jurisdiction, as if such subsection was in collorated in title VII of the Chil Rights Act of 1964 (42 U.S.C. 2000e et seq.), and as if a violation of sub-section (a) was treated as if it was a violation of section, as appropriate, of such Act (42 U.S.C.2000e--2, 2000e--3).

3. DEFINITIONS.-ln this section the terms ''person", "race", and "national origin" have the meanings given the terms in section 701 of the Civil Rights Act of 1964 (42 U.S.C. 2000e).

SEC. 7. EQUAL RIGHTS UNDER THE LAW.

1. IN GENERAL.-No person in the United States shall he subjected to a practice prohibited under section 1977 of the Revised Statutes (42 U.S.C. 1981), based on the person's hair texture or hairstyle, if that hair texture or that hairstyle is commonly associated ·with a particular race or national origin (including a hairstyle in which hair is tightly coiled or tightly curled, locs, cornrows, twists, braids, Bantu knots, and .Afros).

2. ENFORCEMENT.-Suhsection (a) shall be enforced in the same manner and by the same means, including with the same jurisdiction, as if such subsection was incorporated in section 1977 of the Revised Statutes, and as if a violation of subsection (a) was treated as if it was violation of that section 1977.

SEC. 8. RULE OF CONSTRUCTION.

Nothing in this Act shall be constilled to limit definitions of race or national origin under the Civil Rights Act of 1964 (42 U.S.C. 2000a et seq.), the Fair Housing Act (42 U.S.C. 3601 et seq.), or section 1977 of the Revised Statutes (42 U.S.C. 1981).

SEC. 9. DETERMINATION OF BUDGETARY EFFECTS.

The budgetary effects of this Act, for the pm1)ose of complying with the Statutory Pay-As-You-Go Act of 2010, shall be determined by reference to the latest statement titled "Budgetary Effects of PAYGO Legislation" for this Act, submitted for printing in the Congressional Record by the Chairman of the House Budget Committee, provided that such statement has been submitted prior to the vote on passage.

Passed the House of Representatives March 18, 2022.

Attest: CHERYL L. JOHNSON,

Clerk.

Senate Bill No. 188

CHAPTER58

An act to amend Section 2 I2. I of the Education Code, and to amend Section 12926 of the Government Code, relating to discrimination.

[Approved by Governor July 3, 2019. Filed with Secretary of State July 3, 2019.)

LEGISLATIVE COUNSEL'S DIGEST

SB 188, Mitchell. Discrimination: hairstyles.

Existing law states the policy of the State of California to afford all persons in public schools, regardless of their disability, gender, gender identity, gender expression, nationality, race or ethnicity, religion, sexual orientation, or any other specified characteristic, equal rights and opportunities in the educational institutions of the state, and states that the purpose of related existing law is to prohibit acts that are contrary to that policy and to provide remedies therefor. Existing law defines race or ethnicity for these purposes.

Under the California Fair Employment and Housing Act, it is unlawful to engage in specified discriminatory employment practices, including hiring, promotion, and termination based on certain protected characteristics, including race, unless based on a bona fide occupational qualification or applicable security regulations. The act also prohibits housing discrimination based on specified personal characteristics, including race. The act also prohibits discrimination because of a perception that a person has one of those protected characteristics or is associated with a person who has, or is perceived to have, any of those characteristics. Existing law defines terms such as race, religious beliefs, and sex, among others, for purposes of the act.

This bill would provide that the definition of race for these purposes also include traits historically associated with race, including, but not limited to, hair texture and protective hairstyles, and would define protective hairstyles for purposes of these provisions.

The people of the State of Cal!fornia do enact as follows:

SECTION I. The Legislature finds and declares all of the following:

1. The history of our nation is riddled with laws and societal norms that equated "blackness," and the associated physical traits, for example, dark skin, kinky and curly hair to a badge of inferiority, sometimes subject to separate and unequal treatment.

2. This idea also permeated societal understanding of professionalism. Professionalism was, and still is, closely linked to European features and mannerisms, which entails that those who do not naturally fall into Eurocentric norms must alter their appearances, sometimes drastically and permanently, in order to be deemed professional.

3. Despite the great strides American society and laws have made to reverse the racist ideology that Black traits are inferior, hair remains a rampant source of racial discrimination with serious economic and health consequences, especially for Black individuals.

4. Workplace dress code and grooming policies that prohibit natural hair, including afros, braids, twists, and locks, have a disparate impact on Black individuals as these policies are more likely to deter Black applicants and burden or punish Black employees than any other group.

5. Federal courts accept that Title VII of the Civil Rights Act of 1964 prohibits discrimination based on race, and therefore protects against discrimination against afros. However, the courts do not understand that

afros are not the only natural presentation of Black hair. Black hair can also be naturally presented in braids, twists, and locks.

6. In a society in which hair has historically been one of many determining factors of a person's race, and whether they were a second class citizen, hair today remains a proxy for race. Therefore, hair discrimination targeting hairstyles associated with race is racial discrimination.

7. Acting in accordance with the constitutional values offairness, equity, and opportunity for all, the Legislature recognizes that continuing to enforce a Eurocentric image of professionalism through purportedly race-neutral grooming policies that disparately impact Black individuals and exclude them from some workplaces is in direct opposition to equity and opportunity for all.

SEC. 2. Section 212.1 of the Education Code is amended to read:

1. "Race or ethnicity" includes ancestry, color, ethnic group identification, and ethnic background.

2. "Race" is inclusive of traits historically associated with race, including, but not limited to, hair texture and protective hairstyles.

3. "Protective hairstyles" includes, but is not limited to, such hairstyles as braids, locks, and twists.

SEC. 3. Section 12926 of the Government Code is amended to read: 12926. As used in this part in connection with unlawful practices, unless a different meaning clearly appears from the context:

1. "Affirmative relief" or "prospective relief" includes the authority to order reinstatement of an employee, awards of backpay, reimbursement

of out-of-pocket expenses, hiring, transfers, reassignments, grants of tenure, promotions, cease and desist orders, posting of notices, training of personnel, testing, expunging of records, reporting of records, and any other similar relief that is intended to correct unlawful practices under this part.

2. "Age" refers to the chronological age of any individual who has reached a 40th birthday.

3. Except as provided by Section 12926.05, ''employee'' does not include any individual employed by that person's parent, spouse, or child or any individual employed under a special license in a nonprofit sheltered workshop or rehabilitation facility.

4. "Employer" includes any person regularly employing five or more persons, or any person acting as an agent of an employer, directly or indirectly, the state or any political or civil subdivision of the state, and cities, except as follows: "Employer" does not include a religious association or corporation not organized for private profit.

5. "Employment agency" includes any person undertaking for compensation to procure employees or opportunities to work.

"Essential functions" means the fundamental job duties of the employment position the individual with a disability holds or desires. "Essential functions" does not include the marginal functions of the position.

A job function may be considered essential for any of several reasons, including, but not limited to, any one or more of the following:

1. The function may be essential because the reason the position exists is to perform that function.

2. The function may be essential because of the limited number of employees available among whom the performance of that job function can be distributed.

3. The function may be highly specialized, so that the incumbent in the position is hired based on expertise or the ability to perform a particular function.

4. Evidence of whether a particular function is essential includes, but is not limited to, the following

5. The employer's judgment as to which functions are essential.

6. Written job descriptions prepared before advertising or interviewing applicants for the job.

7. The amount of time spent on the job performing the function.

8. The consequences of not requiring the incumbent to perform the function.

9. The terms of a collective bargaining agreement.

10. The work experiences of past incumbents in the job.

11. The current work experience of incumbents in similar jobs.

"Genetic information" means, with respect to any individual, information about any of the following:

1. The individual's genetic tests.

2. The genetic tests of family members of the individual.

3. The manifestation of a disease or disorder in family members of the

individual.

4. "Genetic information" includes any request for, or receipt of, genetic services, or participation in clinical research that includes genetic services, by an individual or any family member of the individual.

5. (3) "Genetic information" does not include information about the sex or age of any individual.

6. "Labor organization" includes any organization that exists and is constituted for the purpose, in whole or in part, of collective bargaining or of dealing with employers concerning grievances, terms or conditions of employment, or of other mutual aid or protection.

"Medical condition" means either of the following:

(I) Any health impairment related to or associated with a diagnosis of cancer or a record or history of cancer.

(2) Genetic characteristics. For purposes of this section, "genetic characteristics" means either of the following:

(A) Any scientifically or medically identifiable gene or chromosome, or combination or alteration thereof, that is known to be a cause of a disease or disorder in a person or that person's offspring, or that is determined to be associated with a statistically increased risk of development of a disease or disorder, and that is presently not associated with any symptoms of any disease or disorder.

(B) Inherited characteristics that may derive from the individual or family member, that are known to be a cause of a disease or disorder in a person or that person's offspring, or that are determined to be associated with a statistically increased risk of development of a disease or disorder, and that are presently not associated with any symptoms of any disease or disorder.

G) "Mental disability" includes, but is not limited to, all of the following:

(I) Having any mental or psychological disorder or condition, such as intellectual disability, organic brain syndrome, emotional or mental illness, or specific learning disabilities, that limits a major life activity. For purposes of this section:

(A) "Limits" shall be determined without regard to mitigating measures, such as medications, assistive devices, or reasonable accommodations, unless the mitigating measure itself limits a major life activity.

(B) A mental or psychological disorder or condition limits a major life activity if it makes the achievement of the major life activity difficult.

(C) "Major life activities" shall be broadly construed and shall include physical, mental, and social activities and working.

(2) Any other mental or psychological disorder or condition not described in paragraph (I) that requires special education or related services.

(3) Having a record or history of a mental or psychological disorder or condition described in paragraph (1) or (2), which is known to the employer or other entity covered by this part.

(4) Being regarded or treated by the employer or other entity covered by this part as having, or having had, any mental condition that makes achievement of a major life activity difficult.

(5) Being regarded or treated by the employer or other entity covered by this part as having, or having had, a mental or psychological disorder or condition that has no present disabling effect, but that may become a mental disability as described in paragraph (1) or (2).

"Mental disability" does not include sexual behavior disorders, compulsive gambling, kleptomania, pyromania, or psychoactive substance use disorders resulting from the current unlawful use of controlled substances or other drugs.

(k) ..Military and veteran status" means a member or veteran of the United States Armed Forces, United States Armed Forces Reserve, the United States National Guard, and the California National Guard.

(/) ..On the bases enumerated in this part" means or refers to discrimination on the basis of one or more of the following: race, religious creed, color, national origin, ancestry, physical disability, mental disability, medical condition, genetic information, marital status, sex, age, sexual orientation, or military and veteran status.

(m) "Physical disability" includes, but is not limited to, all of the following:

(I) Having any physiological disease, disorder, condition, cosmetic disfigurement, or anatomical loss that does both of the following:

(A) Affects one or more of the following body systems: neurological, immunological, musculoskeletal, special sense organs, respiratory, including speech organs, cardiovascular, reproductive, digestive, genitourinary, hemic and lymphatic, skin, and endocrine.

(B) Limits a major life activity. For purposes of this section:

(i) "Limits" shall be determined without regard to mitigating measures such as medications, assistive devices, prosthetics, or reasonable accommodations, unless the mitigating measure itself limits a major life activity.

(ii) A physiological disease, disorder, condition, cosmetic disfigurement, or anatomical loss limits a major life activity if it makes the achievement of the major life activity difficult.

(iii) "Major life activities" shall be broadly construed and includes physical, mental, and social activities and working.

(2) Any other health impairment not described in paragraph (I) that requires special education or related services.

(3) Having a record or history of a disease, disorder, condition, cosmetic disfigurement, anatomical loss, or health impairment described in paragraph

(1) or (2), which is known to the employer or other entity covered by this part.

(4) Being regarded or treated by the employer or other entity covered by this part as having, or having had, any physical condition that makes achievement of a major life activity difficult.

(5) Being regarded or treated by the employer or other entity covered by this part as having, or having had, a disease, disorder, condition,

cosmetic disfigurement, anatomical loss, or health impairment that has no present disabling effect but may become a physical disability as described in paragraph (1) or (2).

(6) "Physical disability" does not include sexual behavior disorders, compulsive gambling, kleptomania, pyromania, or psychoactive substance use disorders resulting from the current unlawful use of controlled substances or other drugs.

(n) Notwithstanding subdivisions G) and (m), if the definition of "disability" used in the federal Americans with Disabilities Act of 1990 (Public Law 101-336) would result in broader protection of the civil rightsof individuals with a mental disability or physical disabi nclude any medical condition not included within those definitions, then that broader protection or coverage shall be deemed incorporated by reference into, and shall prevail over conflicting provisions of, the definitions in subdivisions G) and (m).

(o) "Race, religious creed, color, national origin, ancestry, physical disability, mental disability, medical condition, genetic information, marital status, sex, age, sexual orientation, or military and veteran status" includes a perception that the person has any of those characteristics or that the person is associated with a person who has, or is perceived to have, any of those characteristics.

(p) "Reasonable accommodation" may include either of the following:

(1) Making existing facilities used by employees readily accessible to, and usable by, individuals with disabilities.

(2) Job restructuring, part-time or modified work schedules, reassignment to a vacant position, acquisition or modification of equipment or devices, adjustment or modifications of examinations, training materials or policies, the provision of qualified readers or interpreters, and other similar accommodations for individuals with disabilities

(q) "Religious creed," "religion," "religious observance," "religious belief," and "creed" include all aspects of religious belief, observance, and practice, including religious dress and grooming practices. "Religious dress practice" shall be construed broadly to include the wearing or carrying of religious clothing, head or face coverings, jewelry, artifacts, and any other item that is part of an individual observing a religious creed. "Religious grooming practice" shall be construed broadly to include all forms of head, facial, and body hair that are part of an individual observing a religious creed.

(r) (1) "Sex" includes, but is not limited to, the following:

(A) Pregnancy or medical conditions related to pregnancy.

(B) Childbirth or medical conditions related to childbirth.

(C) Breastfeeding or medical conditions related to breastfeeding.

(2) "Sex" also includes, but is not limited to, a person's gender. "Gender" means sex, and includes a person's gender identity and gender expression. "Gender expression" means a person's gender-related appearance and behavior whether or not stereotypicallyassociated with the person's assigned sex at birth.

(s) "Sexual orientation" means heterosexuality, homosexuality, and bisexuality.

(t) "Supervisor" means any individual having the authority, in the interest of the employer, to hire, transfer, suspend, lay off, recall, promote, discharge, assign, reward, or discipline other employees, or the responsibility to direct them, or to adjust their grievances, or effectively to recommend that action, if, in connection with the foregoing, the exercise of that authority is not of a merely routine or clerical nature, but requires the use of independent judgment.

(u) "Undue hardship" means an action requiring significant difficulty or expense, when considered in light of the following factors:

(1) The nature and cost of the accommodation needed.

(2) The overall financial resources of the facilities involved in the provision of the reasonable accommodations, the number of persons employed at the facility, and the effect on expenses and resources or the impact otherwise of these accommodations upon the operation of the facility.

(3) The overall financial resources of the covered entity, the overall size

of the business of a covered entity with respect to the number of employees, and the number, type, and location of its facilities.

(4) The type of operations, including the composition, structure, and functions of the workforce of the entity.

(5) The geographic separateness or administrative or fiscal relationship of the facility or facilities.

(v) "National origin" discrimination includes, but is not limited to, discrimination on the basis of possessing a driver's license granted under Section 12801.9 of the Vehicle Code.

(w) "Race" is inclusive of traits historically associated with race, including, but not limited to, hair texture and protective hairstyles.

(x) "Protective hairstyles" includes, but is not limited to, such hairstyles as braids, locks, and twists.

ABOUT THE AUTHOR

As a child, growing up in Brooklyn, N.Y., one of six children, I was an avid reader and my world was mostly my "block". On occasions like holidays, we would visit aunts, uncles, grandparents and some summers our parents would pack us up in the car and drive to South Carolina, where our parents and grandparents migrated from.

My "hair journey" began in Bed-Stuy, Brooklyn as the granddaughter of a hairdresser/milliner (Mabel Singleton Ruffins) and the daughter of (Henrietta Singleton King), working mother of five daughters, who entrusted me, her oldest daughter the task of "doing hair" of my younger siblings.

Reading is what took me on my "journey around the world". Which began to occupy my thoughts and dreams about the world that existed beyond "the block". School trips were another advantage which allowed me to realize a world beyond my block, my street, the city and eventually the country.

The 60's, civil rights, Dr. Martin Luther King, Jr., Black Power, Vietnam, JFK... What a pivotal time in the life of this young Black girl (as it was for many others, but this is my story).

Afros, dashikis, Africa (the motherland)... things I was learning about and experiencing beyond my formal public school education. I began to read more and more. By the 1970's, I had somehow morphed into the black girl with "big natural hair", pierced nose, large hoop earrings... Afrocentricity was me. I later met a brother who would mentor and encourage me in all aspects of African art, culture and creativity.

When I graduated from high school, I had one focus, to travel to the "Motherland". I delayed college and in 1973, I was on my way. First time on a plane, first time leaving the country, I was off on a journey of a lifetime to Ghana, West Africa (byway of Amsterdam. Las Palmas, Canary Islands and Liberia).

In the years to follow, I became a wife and a mother, a business owner, a writer/publisher. I returned to Africa several times and was eventually blessed to travel there with my children Akua and Osei-Kwame.

1973-first trip to Africa

1980-published Africa Hairstyles Book I

1981-featured article /N.Y. Amsterdam Newspaper "Heritage of Hairstyles"

1982-founded Akua-Adiki Anokye Publications

1994-published "Braiders Guide I" - A Braiding Resource Guide

1995-published "Braiders Guide II" - Directory of Braiding & Natural Hair Salons

1995-Graduate: Natural Hair Care & Braiding Course - Medgar Evers College, Brooklyn, N.Y.

1996-return to Ghana, West Africa

2012-travelled to Liberia, West Africa

2018 - travelled to Durban, South Africa

African Hairstyles
Book I
by Akua-Adiki Anokye

Smithsonian Libraries and Archives

Object Details

Author: Anokye, Akua-Adiki

1980   C1980

Call number: TT972.A615 1980

TT972.A615 1980

Type: Books

Physical description 31 p.: ill.; 22 cm

Place: Africa

Smithsonian Libraries

Topic: Hairdressing of Blacks Hairdressing

Record ID: siris_si1_375676

Metadata Usage (text)

cco